Mediaballs

All the world's best media rubbish, including:

- **The stupidest quiz show answers**
- **The worst misprints**
- **The most pretentious writers**
- **The silliest actors**

Edited by **Marcus Berkmann**

Illustrated by **Grizelda**

Pickpocket targets elderly women

Midweek Herald, Devon

Published in Great Britain
by Private Eye Productions Ltd,
6 Carlisle Street, London W1D 3BN

©2003 Pressdram Ltd
ISBN 1 901784 33 9
Designed by Bridget Tisdall
Printed in Great Britain by
Cox and Wyman Ltd, Reading

DUMB BRITAIN

Real contestants, real quiz shows, real answers, real dumb

Steve Wright: What is the Italian word for motorway?
Contestant: Expresso.

BBC Radio 2

Anne Robinson: An injection of cash given to an ailing business is referred to as a shot into which part of the body?
Contestant: The dark.

The Weakest Link

Grant Stott: Who is the leader of the Ulster Unionist Party?
Contestant: Geri Halliwell.

Radio Forth

Anne Robinson: Who wrote the political treatise Das Kapital?
Contestant: John Major.

The Weakest Link

Steve Penk: What is the name of the French-speaking Canadian state?
Contestant: America? Portugal? Canada? Mexico? Italy? Spain?

Virgin Radio

Anne Robinson: Which Indian leader, whose last name began with 'G', took the title Mahatma?
Contestant: Geronimo.

The Weakest Link

Steve Wright: Who played the lead character in the 1961 movie *El Cid*?
Contestant: Charles Hawtrey.

BBC Radio 2

Anne Robinson: Which of the Marx Brothers remained silent throughout all their movies?
Contestant: Karl.

The Weakest Link

Anne Robinson: Which British politician is credited with founding the Metropolitan Police while he was Home Secretary?
Contestant: Douglas Hurd.

The Weakest Link

Steve Lefevre: What was signed to bring the First World War to an end in 1918?
Contestant: The Magna Carta.

The Biggest Game In Town, ITV

William G. Stewart: What major town on the River Severn, famed for its fine china, shares its name with the sauce used in a Bloody Mary?
Contestant: Tomato.

Fifteen To One, C4

Anne Robinson: Which composer wrote The Magic Flute?
Contestant: Bikini.

The Weakest Link

Paul Ross: What is the name of the Israeli Secret Service?
Contestant: I'll make an educated guess. The FBI.
No Win No Fee, BBC1

Anne Robinson: The presenter of the television series *Telly Addicts* was Noel who?
Contestant: Coward.

The Weakest Link

Steve Allen: What does the Celtic name Conan mean?
Contestant: Barbarian.

LBC

Nigel Lythgoe: Who was the 20th-century Israeli general-turned-politician who always wore an eye patch?
Contestant: Nelson.
Another contestant: Yasser Arafat.

The Enemy Within, BBC1

Anne Robinson: Which British leading man played opposite Celia Johnson in the film *Brief Encounter*?
Contestant: James Dean.

The Weakest Link

Anne Robinson: The site of a famous battle in the English Civil War, the village of Naseby is 20 miles south of which British city?
Contestant: Southampton.

The Weakest Link

Anne Robinson: Which famous artist painted the Mona Lisa?
Contestant: Frank Bough.

The Weakest Link

Chris Searle: In which European country is Mount Etna?
Contestant: Japan.
Chris Searle: I did say which European country, so in case you didn't hear that, I can let you try again.
Contestant: Er... Mexico.

BBC Radio Bristol

Anne Robinson: What 'T' are people who live in a house paying rent to a landlord?
Contestant: Terrorists.

The Weakest Link

Anne Robinson: Who was the only inmate of Spandau Prison in Berlin between 1966 and 1987?
Contestant: The Birdman of Alcatraz.

The Weakest Link

Anne Robinson: In Scotland, which river flows past Balmoral Castle?
Contestant: The Thames.

The Weakest Link

Anne Robinson: Which calendar month is named after the first Roman Emperor, Caesar Augustus?
Contestant: June.

The Weakest Link

John Leslie: On which river is Newcastle situated?
Contestant: The Thames.
Leslie: Yes. Well done!

This Morning, ITV

Nigel Lythgoe: Which of the Seven Wonders of the Ancient World would you have found in Babylon?
Contestant: The Hanging Baskets.

The Enemy Within, BBC1

Anne Robinson: Who was Prime Minister when England won the World Cup in 1966?
Contestant: Woodrow Wilson.

The Weakest Link

Presenter: In which direction do the hands of a clock travel?
Contestant: Anti-clockwise.

GMTV

Steve Wright: To which English king was Guinevere married?
Contestant *(after long pause to think)*: Henry VIII.

BBC Radio 2

Anne Robinson: In which country is the river Po?
Contestant: Poland.

The Weakest Link

William G Stewart: Which city in Devon lies at the southern end of the M5 motorway?
Contestant: Southern Yemen.

Fifteen To One, C4

Les Dennis: Name an excuse that might be given for why a train is late.
Contestant: It's been delayed.

Family Fortunes, ITV

Janice Forsyth: What is the currency in India?
Contestant: Ramadan.

BBC Radio Scotland

Anne Robinson: What 'K' is the currency of Sweden?
Contestant: Kennel.

The Weakest Link

A penny farthing bicycle similar to this one was stolen from the Rathfriland man's home. It is worth around £1,500

Sunday Life

K. CHRISTMAS PUDDING CHARMS

Sterling silver charms to bring good fortune. Potential choking hazard: do not use with food.

Past Times

And today, police are carrying out house-to-house injuries in a bid to find out the identity of the firestarters.

South Wales Argus

A pat on the back to the council.

Whenever we go to Ramsgate the toilets are clean, and the seats are just right for viewing the sea and wonderful harbour.

Isle of Thanet Gazette

"Washington officials told news network CNN they have intelligence evidence that ties the Algerians to Zarqawi, a one-legged Jordanian who commanded an al Qaeda training camp in Afghanistan and is now on the run."

www.thisislondon.co.uk

LUVVIES

Gems from the acting profession

"I think it's really bloody important to show birth like that, before pain control and epidurals, just like in all the damn agony. If Thomas Hardy were alive today, he'd be kissing Michael Winterbottom's feet."

Kate Winslet on Winterbottom's screen adaptation of *Jude The Obscure*

"Leo knows he's got sex appeal and he knows how to use it. Yet he doesn't think that he's gorgeous. And to me he's simply smelly, farty Leo."

Kate Winslet on Leonardo DiCaprio

"That's the thing I noticed about Nick years ago," says his friend Jim Carrey, who met Cage ten years back on the set of *Peggy Sue Got Married*. "He doesn't just pick up a wedge of cheese. He wants to know the history. He wants to know exactly who made the cheese."

Jim Carrey on Nicolas Cage, *Vanity Fair*

"It [the word 'luvvies'] is a word that's had a deadly impact. I think it's a word that's as appalling and as abhorrent as any racist word. I hope I choose my words carefully and without the hyperbole that's supposed to be the affliction of the luvvie, but I think it's as disgusting as the word 'yid' or 'nigger'."

Trevor Nunn, *Vogue*

"Vanity was a big issue, a big sin in our family, so anything self-regarding or narcissistic was wicked, and choosing to be an actress was the *ultimate*. That's probably why I didn't like it at first. But now I just love having a piece of paper with black and white stuff on it and having to turn that into flesh and blood. It's practically religious..."

Kristin Scott-Thomas, *Time Out*

"I picked it up [the script for *Bodyguard II*] and the first 30 pages were totally her. It was dignified, sexy, smart, funny. And I couldn't finish. It broke my heart."

Kevin Costner on his proposed co-starring role with Princess Diana

Actor John Goodman has been winning rave reviews for his portrayal of Falstaff in an American stage production of Shakespeare's *Henry IV*. But he admits the role is tough going. He said, "It is not like falling off a bicycle. It's like trying to drag a bicycle up Mount McKinley."

Exeter Express & Echo

"I was so used up. I said I honestly don't know if I can do it again. She said, 'Let me give you my strength.' She took my hands in hers, and she just looked at me. We stood there with the crew working around us, and she just looked at me. I don't know what she was thinking, maybe the laundry list, but I saw in her eyes, she let me see who she was, the fears, the pain, everything... and I started crying. She stepped back, and we did it another time."

Barbara Hershey on Jane Campion

Ben Kingsley: We discover every day that we work on this play [*Waiting For Godot*] that it is much bigger than it was yesterday.
Alan Howard: Infinite.
Ben Kingsley: There are circles within circles. The circles are as big as the theatre, as big as London, and then they start to nudge the stars.

Guardian

"It was so heartless. I just loved playing Tinky Winky. I really understood him and got into the role... I've never felt such rejection... They told me they wanted me to say eh-oo in a high-pitched voice, then at the last second they wanted it in a low voice which gave me no time to prepare. Playing Tinky Winky was much more physically demanding than any Shakespeare... I really threw myself into the character... I was always the one to test out the limitations of the costume. I was the first to fall off my chair and roll over. I took all the risks."

Dave Thompson on his sacking from *Teletubbies*

"I wanted to get off this nice mattress of comedy and have a go at lying on the bed of nails of drama."

Rebecca Front, *Telegraph Magazine*

"Beyond its entertainment value, *Baywatch* has enriched and, in many cases, helped save lives. I'm looking forward to the opportunity to continue with a project which has had such significance for so many."

David Hasselhoff, *Pittsburgh Post-Gazette*

"Hobbies include: Swimming, tennis, motorbikes, body-piercing and her animals.

Vanessa would like to thank Performers (agency) and dedicates her performance in *Chicago* to the eight most important people in her life (you know who you are!). Thank you for your belief, love, tears and encouragement and for putting up with my temper tantrums. I love you."

Vanessa Leagh-Hicks, programme notes, *Chicago*

"Actually, when I first met Eric [Cantona] I had no idea who he was. Fortunately, Richard Attenborough saved the day. He told me, 'Darling, haven't you seen him play soccer? He's a god.' So I watched Eric on video, and I thought, yes, he's got an amazing intuitive ability to know where the ball is and it's the kind of intuition you need as an actor."

Cate Blanchett, *Express*

"It's the first time I've been on stage for 15 years... I was so scared it was literally like going in front of a firing squad."

Bob Hoskins, *Parkinson*

"Hollywood can be very heartless. Every year you work in Hollywood takes a year off your soul."

Calista Flockhart, *Bristol Evening Post*

"It is easy for celebrities to forget the importance of 'giving back'; but if, like me, you get into the swing of charitable works, you soon find yourself addicted to compassion, which is now the essential nutrient of my soul."

Michael Bolton, *Billboard*

"For some reason or other I ended up the biggest TV star in the world and it's hard to stop because, if I don't go to work, *Baywatch* dies."

David Hasselhoff, *Hello!*

Winslet found the 'death' scene particularly taxing. "It's all very well to lie there with your eyes closed and white make-up all over your face, but to make it believable you have to believe you are dying. It was like hallucinating. I went into a place in my soul I never knew existed. I went inside a black box that I couldn't get out of, and it was like my soul and my spirit had turned into some bizarre heavy substance between coal and lead. Scary."

Kate Winslet, *Sunday Times Magazine*

"We went in alone at the end of a hugely hectic day, and John [Malkovich] just spoke a few lines and began to weep. I started to weep. I looked over at Leonardo, and tears were just streaming down his face. We were looking at each other like, my God, we have seen the king, and Leo said, 'I don't think I want to do this scene. I think I just want to go back and get in bed and cry for a couple of hours.'"

Randall Wallace, director, on filming
The Man In The Iron Mask

"Whatever it is that dictates the individual about you is the one thing you should keep. I don't wear eyeliner any more, but the bit of me that did is the bit that I lost for a while and that I've been desperately clawing my way back towards."

Rufus Sewell, *Sunday Times Magazine*

"I'm just trying to say that I think it's going to get harder and harder if people don't start treating actors in this country with respect a little bit more... I think actors are far more reluctant, and particularly when people like Alan and Helen receive such maulings in the press, I have to say. Some of it was so personal it made me really angry. They put their careers on the line, they do. They don't need to do that, we don't need to do it. We do it because we love it."

Robert Lindsay, *The Independent*

THE cast of My Fair Lady get together to celebrate the 40th anniversary of the making of the film

Halifax Courier

October is a time for self-help...
Low Self Esteem Support Group will meet Thursday at 7 PM. Please use the back door.

St Peter's Church, St Leonards-on-Sea

FILM director Michael Winner was in intensive care last night after a heart scare.

Fifteen-stone Winner was put under 24-hour observation by cardiac doctors, fearing he might suffer dangerous internal bleeding. Winner's girlfriend Geraldine Lynton-Edwards said: "We are all very happy about it.

Daily Mirror

A bullied teacher has been awarded a £230,000 payout for personal injury and loss of earnings after being forced out of his job by his head.

Grauniad

Earth Summit 'offers no help for east Kent'

East Kent Mercury

8.00 Danger In The Skies (S,T)
See above.

Metro

'Fayed's chopper drives us crazy'

Ealing & Acton Gazette

THE NEOPHILIACS
──── 2001 ────

"Busking seems to be the new rock 'n' roll."
Richard Morrison, *The Times*

"Sushi – it's the new rock 'n' roll."
Vicki Tagg, *Bristol Evening Post*

"In the wake of the huge American success of The Mummy Returns, the question has inevitably arisen: why are we so fascinated with mummies? Is it a Freud thing, or a fashion statement – bandages as the new black?"
Cosmo Landesman, *Sunday Times*

"Cricket's mass-marketing is long overdue. The premise that the sport of gentlemen can become the new rock 'n' roll is entirely plausible."
Hannah Betts, *The Times*

"Art... the new rock 'n' roll."
Rachel Campbell-Johnston, *The Times*

"Domesticity is the new rock 'n' roll. Or, to put it another way, it's in to stay in."
Virginia Backbrun, *Daily Mail*

"We have a throwaway attitude to everything else, so why not pets?... So too bad for terrapins if they are no longer the new black."
Geraldine Bedell, *The Independent*

"If gardening is the new sex then Hampton Court Flower Show must be a major erogenous zone."
Patricia Cleveland-Peck, *Independent On Sunday*

"Socialism for Scotland is the new rock 'n' roll."
Angus Calder, *Guardian*

"Nigella has made cooking the new sex."
Hadley Freeman, *Guardian*

"Staying in seems to be the new going out."
Lee Holmes, *Independent On Sunday*

"Going out is the new going out."
Barometer trends column, *Daily Mail*

"Fashion: Small is the New Big."
The Times

"The trendsetters were all drinking vodka mixed with fizzy pop or cranberry juice... Cranberry is the new black."
Mick Hume, *The Times*

Dianaballs

"Just two months after the death of Diana, Princess of Wales, a German university has made her the subject of an academic course. The series of 14 lectures will focus on the myth and meaning of her life and will be taught by the politics department at Berlin University... Students will take part in seminars such as 'Diana, A Latter Day Virgin Mary', 'Emotion As A Political Weapon' and even 'Diana, Priestess Of The Cult Of Victimhood'."

BBC Radio News

"Mix the Beanie Baby collection craze with the Princess Diana memorabilia rush and pandemonium is assured. Princess, a cuddly royal purple bear in memory of Diana, is due in selected stores in the next two weeks... Princess comes with a customised Beanie Baby poem attached:

> *Like an angel, she came from heaven above*
> *She shared her compassion, her pain, her love*
> *She only stayed with us long enough to teach*
> *The world to share, to give, to reach."*

USA Today

"Working it out recently, I calculated that I'd had 40 sexual partners in the month following Princess Diana's funeral. Not since her death – nothing during that first week – but since the funeral on the following Saturday. All safe sex, and I include a few threesomes... This particular death briefly abolished loneliness because suddenly everyone had a route into everyone else."

Duncan Fallowell, *Evening Standard*

"Our sincere thanks to the folks at Rhode Island Soft Systems for producing the beautifully done tribute that honours such a special woman. Using 20 stunning photographs, all licensed from the UPI, this screen-saver will capture your heart and help you remember Diana."

Advert on Compuserve's bulletin board, December 1997

"In her treatise 'That's The Way The Mercedes Benz: Di, Wound Culture and Fatal Fetishism', Diane Rubinstein describes how Diana 'functions as a radical fetish of virtual reality, a move beyond alienation to a principle of otherness raised to technical perfection'. She sees the Mercedes car in which Diana was fatally injured in Paris as a 'psychotopography of interior spaces' and her wounds as 'so many new sexual organs opened on the body'. The princess's fatality 'erupts in the *mise en scène* of her body and its erotogeneity', she concludes."

Sunday Times

"*Gay Demokratische Neurosen*. Known for his graphic illustrations of male rape and gay porn, taboo-busting artist Martin von Ostrowski presents a new collection of works devoted to 'Neuroses of Democracy'. Executed in brightly coloured oils and chalk, they include a portrait of Princess Diana, 'Diana war eine von uns' (Diana was one of us), which depicts a smiling princess whose lips, nose, ears and cheekbones are all extensively pierced. Until 24 April. Mon-Fri 9am-5pm."

Exhibition listing in *Time Out*

"Well done – the supplement on Diana, Princess of Wales was so tastefully handled. And it wasn't just placed inside the magazine to fall out all over the floor, but was sealed in a plastic cover. I think it showed the respect she so rightly deserved."

Letter in *Bella*

11.05 Real Sex. Action from a crucial title showdown match in the Eredivisie. With PSV Eindhoven, Ajax and Feyenoord all in contention, who will be crowned champions? (R) 4492742

Scottish Sunday Herald

Passengers to wait 10 years for fast trains

The Times

Blairism (E6)

See also: **Thatcherism**

Routledge Dictionary of Economics

■ **Councillor Mike Pullon:** calling for action.

■ **Councillor Tony Potts:** satisfied customer.

The Citizen, Gloucester

Condon's pledge to murder witnesses

By STEPHEN WRIGHT
Crime Correspondent

Daily Mail

Leadership decided by secret ballet

East Lindsey Target

O·B·N

Awarded for services to toadyism and bootlicking

"According to a survey in Red magazine, women feel that they're failures because they don't live up to Nigella Lawson.

"They shouldn't worry because no one could live up to Nigella.

"She's breathtakingly beautiful with a perfect figure. She's a marvellous cook, an emotional rock to her clever husband, John Diamond, writes two weekly columns, works like a navvy, makes irresistible TV series and produces bestsellers as well as perfect cakes.

"She's kind and very funny. I'm afraid she's also terribly nice."

Lynda Lee-Potter, *Daily Mail*

Simon Mayo: If you ran the country, who would you put on the stamps?
Trevor Kavanagh (of *The Sun*): Rupert Murdoch. He's a hero of mine.

Radio 5 Live

"Although committed to her musical career – 'I really enjoy the whole process of making music,' she recently told me – Victoria [Beckham] remains the most famous and sought-after female celebrity in Britain; able, if she chooses, to divert her career into television or film with just one phone call."

Martin Townsend, *Sunday Express*

"Yesterday, one Sunday paper had a list of the 300 most beautiful women 'of all time'. For some reason, it did not contain a picture of Joanna Trollope, who was photographed in another of the papers in a split skirt going all the way to the top of her beautiful thighs... Joanna is easily more beautiful than many of the so-called lovelies of all time."

A.N. Wilson, *Evening Standard*

"Did you know that there are only four years between Madonna, the Princess of Pop, and Cherie, the Diva of Downing Street?"

Lauren Booth, *New Statesman*

"Nigella Lawson was pictured at the weekend looking alluring in a blonde wig. Since then there has been endless discussion about whether she looks more beautiful as a blonde or brunette. The discussion is academic because Nigella would look divine even if she dyed her lustrous hair purple and encased her shapely, perfect body in baggy orange Crimplene. Nigella could probably even make Crimplene seem stylish."

Lynda Lee-Potter, *Daily Mail*

Pseuds
Corner

Pretentious media-related tripe from the Eye's most venerable column

"[Nicolas] Cage can do more by simply exhaling than any actor in movie history; with one nearly silent expulsion of breath, he can express all the existential disappointment of European philosophy."

Andrew O'Hehir, *Salon*

"Günter Grass – The pain that runs through my being."

Strapline on front page of *Guardian*

"London rain often feels like piss, because it hasn't too far to fall from the lowering sky. The London pedestrian finds himself crawling along the gutter-like streets, while some down-and-out deity pisses on him from a modest height. Or so I thought, dropping into Boots to buy an apple-flavoured breakfast bar. I munched it under the pediment of the political bookshop and sucked in a desultory fashion on a roll-up with the approximate length and density of a feline penis."

Will Self, *Independent On Sunday*

"You're standing in thigh-high grass that glimmers like brushed satin and stretches out voluptuously to the horizon, basking in birdsong and the wind's seaside whisper. Suddenly you hear a roar building behind you: a little bi-plane shoots overhead, throwing loops in the bright blue sky, showing off. You watch it, amazed. A couple of local kids tumble up and stare at it, then stare at you as if your nose is green. Three scraggy dogs follow them, barking maniacally. The noisy scene fills you with the desire to throw your head back and laugh at its absurdity, laugh until your stomach is stiff.

"Picture that and you'll have a small idea of the joy waiting for you in NoahJohn's second album."

Maddy Costa, *Guardian*

"But when I demurred and said that I think anorexia is a latent obsessive-compulsive disorder that's potentiated by this kind of culturally promulgated fixation with body image, Twiggy crowed, 'You're right, actually!' Which is refreshing, because usually when I say things of this form, people look a little nonplussed."

Will Self, *Independent On Sunday*

"When I met Damien [Hirst], ten or eleven years ago, I knew right away he was going to be the next Andy Warhol. He was dirty and sexy and rude. I said, 'Hello, I'm Isabella,' and he said, 'Hello, you fucking cunt.' So I knew something was going on."

Isabella Blow, *New Yorker*

"I have always believed that education fuels and drives progress in our society – which is why I go on teaching. An evening at King's reassured me that we academics are still on target to change the world."

Lisa Jardine, The Times

"It's hard to be single. We all had the experience of we could've married the guy who was the wrong guy for the sake of being married and we didn't. There is something noble in that and there is something noble in taking care of yourself and becoming fully actualised as a human being."

Candace Bushnell, Spectrum
(Scotland On Sunday magazine)

"It is disconcerting, when talking of Russian literature, to generate an original idea or spout an apposite quotation, only to find a week later that you have subconsciously purloined it from a long-forgotten reading of Prince Dimitri Svyatopolk-Mirsky's History Of Russian Literature (1927)."

Donald Rayfield, Times Literary Supplement

"Cosmetic-polemic/Distinguished by relics/Destructive aesthetic/Intravenous agnostic/Intravenous agnostic/Intravenous agnostic/Intravenous agnostic/Intravenous."

Manic Street Preachers, chorus of
'Intravenous Agnostic'

"The moment Ivo was born, he instantly leapt above getting into Oxford on my list of Best Things That Have Ever Happened To Me, ahead of getting my first novel published and being seduced by an older woman on a beach in Greece."

James Delingpole on fatherhood, *Evening Standard*

"The bathroom is personal space, political space, psychic space. It is also a place of ritual and rebirth, of intimacy and vulnerability; the place we know ourselves both as base and divine, of earth and heaven. It is where we arrive at big decisions after misty meditation and stand naked before God and full-length mirrors."

i-D bathroom issue

"[Alain] de Botton's vision is entirely his own. Who else would observe that the cry of a black-eared wheatear has no effect on a caterpillar 'walking strenuously across a rock'? Has nobody else ever noticed that the texture of Amsterdam brickwork is like that of halva from a Lebanese delicatessen?"

Jan Morris (on Alain de Botton's
The Art Of Travel), *New Statesman*

BLACK JACKET

Sadness isn't sadness
It's happiness
in a black jacket

Death isn't death
it's life
that's jumped off a tall cliff

Tears are not tears
They're balls
of laughter
dipped in salt

Paul McCartney (from *Blackbird Singing:
Poetry and Lyrics 1965-1999*)

"Service was convivial yet unfailingly attentive, and the food the culinary equivalent of full-on, exhibitionist sex with a first date, who then does your laundry."

Marion McGilvary, *the business*
(*FT Weekend* magazine)

Selling big porkies: Sausage-maker Dave Lang with his wife Debbie

Dave Lang and family, livestock farmer, Bath

The Times

Weight Watchers will meet at 7pm at the First Presbyterian Church. Please use the large double door at the side entrance.

Hazel Grove Methodist Church newsletter

Dianaballs

"On my way to the Chanel show, I tried to leave the Ritz by the Rue Cambon entrance, only to find that it was locked and bolted. A bellman showed me a way out through a door into a back-hall anteroom which had a door to the street. It seemed eerily familiar. Jonathan Becker, who was with me, said, 'Isn't this the Princess Diana exit?' '*Oui*,' replied the bellman. We all looked at one another in a Princess Diana moment."

Dominick Dunne, Vanity Fair

"A weekend in a Welsh country retreat is being held for people who can't get over the death of Princess Diana. Therapists have been lined up to comfort people still struggling to come to terms with the tragedy... People going to the seminar are asked to bring a pair of scissors and newspaper pictures of Diana. One of the sessions will involve making a pinboard of pictures."

Western Mail

"Stick a set of Diana stamps on a strip of cardboard from a tights pack and trim to shape to make a lovely bookmark."

Readers' tips in Best magazine

"The latest Princess Diana Phonecard Set marks the first anniversary of this tragic event. The 14 cards show new designs and are all valid for 10 units of call time. Only 2,000 Collections issued worldwide! Free Soccer card with every mail order for all 3 sets!"
Ad in International Numismatics, Singapore

"Confident and arrogant, the men behind the
ruling hand
Descended on Diana like an eagle on a dove.
Virginally suitable, so dutiful, so beautiful,
An innocent aristocrat inside a velvet glove.

Moulding her and scolding her, they set about
enfolding her,
Enmeshing her in protocol like spiders with a fly,
Arranging her, deranging her, they failed to see the
change in her
But smiled in secret victory when the public saw
her cry...

Underestimation of the feelings of a nation
Brought about the slaughter of the eagle by the
dove
The girl they thought so biddable was womanhood,
formidable
In death they found a diamond fist inside the velvet
glove."

'The Puppetmasters' by Sarah Ridgely, a winning entry from Writing magazine's 'Diana: Write Your Own Tribute' competition, as judged by Jeffrey Archer

"Prince William's and Prince Harry's 'touching personal statement' to the nation calling for an end to public mourning for the Princess of Wales aroused my anger. I deeply resent being addressed upon such a deeply felt matter by two very young people. The millions of words that have been written and read over the past 12 months attest to the fact that a vast number of people are still trying to define Diana, to understand what our relationship with her was all about... Would the Princess have encouraged her sons to put their feelings above those of others?"

Letter in *Daily Mail*

"As the nation prepares to mourn the first anniversary of the tragic loss of the People's Princess, surely the People's Premier, Tony Blair, could enshrine the true feelings of the British. There would be no better tribute than renaming the country of her birth Northamptonshire, 'Dianashire'. *Allan Pearcey, London N3.*"

Letter on ITV Teletext

"*Live And Let Di*, written and directed by Catherine McCargo, is set in the early hours of 31 August 1997. Unable to sleep, one by one the Jackson family gather in the living room to watch TV as the news filters through from Paris that Diana, Princess of Wales, has been involved in a car accident. The tension reaches a climax as Steve, the son, considers whether or not to 'come out' to his father."

Programme for Lyric Theatre, Belfast

"Princess Diana License – Exact replica of Diana's official driver's license; it has Diana's height, weight, date of birth and hair color, plus palace address w/color photo. This valuable collector's item can be yours for only $9.95 + $1.00 S&H."

Ad in *Village Voice*, New York

"The Dianameter counts, as a symbol of grief and mourning, the seconds since Princess Diana's tragic death on August 31, 1997."

Application that could be installed on
Palm Pilot electronic organiser

"The 'Mythical Diana Ring' is the symbol of an exceptional woman and the symbol of supreme sophistication. It's patterned after Diana's engagement ring and... contains a genuine sapphire... As soon as you wear this ring, it draws attention and arouses admiration.
Cost: $19.95, $4.50 S&H."

USA Today

"The World's Most Loved Adorable Angel, Free At Last. Consider the heavenly possibilities: a super-realistic animated feature film, *Princess Diana Saves The World*. Equity available, studio participation welcome."

Ad in *Variety*

SAMAK: A family man who rarely misses family dinner.

The Nation, Thailand

Website

Sandra Gidley was promoted
to the Shadow cabinet as
spokesman for women.

Independent

Peterborough Evening Telegraph reader offer

Evening Sentinel, Stoke-on-Trent

LUVVIES

"I bet you're worried. I was worried. That's why I began this piece. I was worried about the vaginas. I was worried about what we think about vaginas, and even more worried that we don't think about them. I was worried about my own vagina. It needed a context of other vaginas – a community, a culture of vaginas."

Eve Ensler in *The Vagina Monologues*

"Celebrity is bestial. It is the worst form of Karma, because of the huge solitude it brings. You are like a gazelle that finds itself straying from the flock. Soon your path is cut off by lions."

Brad Pitt, *Empire*

"Relationships are difficult. It's life. You love life, so you fight. You fight because you love. Otherwise you wouldn't fight. You work. You don't want to die. Why life is a fight I don't know, but gosh! it is."

Sophie Marceau, *Sunday Times Magazine*

"Samantha [Morton] and Rupert [Graves] got some coloured paint," producer Chris Mulburn tells me, "stuck their hands in it and then did hand prints all over the walls of the cottage. They did one wall and then invited me to join in which I didn't think was such a good idea. I spent quite some time explaining to the owner of the cottage that it was a creative thing where actors need to express themselves."

Londoner's Diary, *Evening Standard*

"We wanted a crew that would be able to talk. We wanted huggers. I remember we had to choose between two people who were both really good. Tim [Roth] went, 'I think she'll be a better hugger.'"

Dixie Linder, *Guardian*

"[The scene] was shot over two or three days when Matt [Damon] was aiming for his lowest weight. At the end of the second day he had a pizza standing by so he could eat. But we didn't finish the scene. It was so sad and he couldn't eat the whole thing the next night. That's bravery."

Gwyneth Paltrow, *News Of The World*

"I don't work for the sake of working, it has to be a love affair. Something where desire is very strong because, you know, keeping that feeling alight over a 10-week shoot is sort of like holding an orgasm for three months."

Charlotte Rampling, *Guardian*

"I'd had enough of EastEnders. I felt I'd been taking in toxins for a long while and now I was breathing it all out."

Martine McCutcheon, *Observer*

"I have at times felt like a grief mop as an actor. Not a grief mop for someone else's grief but a grief mop in that I have to scoop out and wipe down my own grief to put it on film."

Nicolas Cage, *Salon* magazine

"I would like to be Jupiter, and lie down in the firmament and make love to everybody."

Roberto Benigni on winning the Oscar for Best Actor

Warballs
9/11

"Bin Laden does not even have to speak. His icon so potently embodies his cause. The irony is that if children were asked to draw Christ, they would draw Bin Laden – not just because of how he dresses, but for his whole demeanour. His is the look of Christ-like suffering, with the intense sexual ambiguity that goes with it. He looks like someone who has suffered an earlier psychological wound... He looks like a victim, languidly feminine, but with his gun over his shoulder he viciously repudiates this femininity and embraces machismo."

Ros Coward, *Guardian*

"Life is 'too short' to put off buying that dream yacht... Since 11 September and the terrorist attacks on America, potential dream boat buyers are no longer: instead they are dream boat buyers!"

Yachting Monthly

"It was a tough week. I found out I was pregnant, Bing and I split up, I gave up smoking, alcohol and coffee, and then 11 September happened. My world collapsed and then the whole world collapsed."

Elizabeth Hurley in *Harper's Bazaar*

"One of the more reassuring pictures post-11 September was of Victoria Beckham at a fashion show in Milan. Her face glowed with a yearning to spend money. I felt that only she stood between us and recession."

Sarah Sands, *Vogue*

"Lorraine Heggessey [controller of BBC1] could not have chosen a more epic moment for her Bafta lecture. The day before, millions watched live on television as terrorists wrought havoc in the United States. The day after, the government gave the thumbs down to the BBC for a digital youth channel."

Bafta Magazine

"Thank goodness October is here. September was a horrifying month. Life is precious and to see it brutally taken away from so many people is not only shocking and tragic but also incredibly unjust. The human race has enough challenges without deliberate efforts to cause misery and mayhem... On a brighter note, Crouch End is fast becoming a trendy rival to Islington's Upper Street."

Editorial in *Alley*, free magazine distributed in Crouch End and Muswell Hill

"*Talk* magazine, the glossy monthly launched just over two years ago by Britain's super-editor in America, Tina Brown, is to close immediately... Staff at the magazine's offices in Manhattan learned of the decision yesterday evening. Ms Brown, who edited the magazine, and its president, Ron Galotti, said that the events of 11 September had condemned the title to an early grave. 'We all had to recognise that 9-11 changed everything,' they said in a brief statement. 'It made it virtually impossible for a stand-alone title like *Talk*.'"

The Independent

"Let's also remember that in America, in the aftermath of 11 September, one of the most often cited routines of daily life that people missed and wanted back was (dare I say it?) advertising."

Allen Rosenshine, chairman and CEO of BBDO Worldwide, *Campaign* magazine

"It's all about texture and tone. The look is still architectural and I've kept a stainless steel oven and hob – essential for hygiene – but I feel stainless steel feels far too clinical, especially after 11 September."

Designer florist Stephen Woodhams on redesigning his kitchen, *Financial Times*

"These businessmen and women go to the 'in' restaurants, but shun the main meals. Instead they plump straight for dessert. 'It reminds them of being a child,' says [lifestyle consultant] Martin Raymond. 'They feel comforted and since 11 September that's been a big issue. It's about pleasure, revenge and sticky toffee pudding.'"

Feature on 'Trunch: The New Lunch', *Mail On Sunday*

"Get ready for another baby boom in summer 2002. This one might not be as big as the post-World War II phenomenon, but demographics experts expect an uptick in the birthrate as a result of 11 September... Consider revamping your line of new baby [flower] arrangements and gifts or just tailoring ads to highlight them – there might be more takers than usual this summer."

Floral Management magazine

"It may be because we live in uncertain times, but we can't seem to get enough of tweed and tartan."

Style column in *Guardian Weekend*, January 2002

"Despite the pundits' gloomy predictions and the inevitable despondency after 11 September, Yorkshire still seems to be bucking all trends and continuing to flourish."

Yorkshire Post

"The Starbucks coffee chain has removed a poster from more than 3,000 cafés in the US and Canada because its picture of a dragonfly hovering beside two big cups of iced tea reminded some customers of the terrorist attack on the World Trade Centre... 'As a responsible company, we want to ensure that nobody is offended,' its spokeswoman said, adding that no customers had complained directly to the company about the advertising campaign."

Guardian

"Matt Damon is to star as Superman in a new movie that sees the Man of Steel battle against Batman. Director Wolfgang Petersen says, 'It is a clash of the Titans. Everything after 11 September is different.'"

The Sun, July 2002

"Alex undoubtedly adds a sprinkling of glamour to the *Big Brother* house as the resident model with the drop dead gorgeous looks. His big break came when he was chosen by Armani for their campaign last autumn, but the tragedy of 11 September meant his face went largely unnoticed."

OK! magazine

"I have hardly been back in the office since the spring/summer shows and here we are debating the creative direction for autumn/winter 2002. It's a tough call: 11 September has transformed everything. How will people view fashion in the future? Too frivolous? After much debate we call our directive for autumn 'Alive!'"

Susanne Tide-Frater, *Vogue*

"How Sept 11 affected plan for bus shelters"

Headline in *Chichester Observer*

"Such strong contributions by marketing to business performance are to be applauded. At-home consumption of lagers also leapt immediately after the events of 11 September in the US. In an uncertain political and economic world that contribution deserves greater recognition."

Editorial in *Marketing* magazine

"But just how do pervs view our changing world, especially after the events of 11 September? Has the sense many of us have that the outside world is now a much scarier place had any significant impact on our internal politics or our enthusiasm for the pursuit of the kinky life?"

Skin Two fetish magazine

Advertisement, Viz

Top of the World Observatories, World Trade Center, Tower 2 ☎323-2340. Two observation decks, on the 107th and 110th floors, indoors and outdoors. The only thing you can't see from here is the future. *NY Pages, City Guide, 2000*

People in Cornwall face more exposure than BNFL staff

IT'S SAFER AT SELLAFIELD

The pace bowler still hopes, however, to make the Ashes tour. "I want to play badly," he said.

Daily Telegraph

British Nuclear Fuels News

DUMB and DUMBER BRITAIN

Anne Robinson: Ken Follett is a famous what, author or photographer?
Contestant: Authotographer.

The Weakest Link

Anne Robinson: Which Douglas lost both legs but still flew in the Battle of Britain?
Contestant: Douglas Hurd.

The Weakest Link

Anne Robinson: What insect is commonly found hovering above lakes?
Contestant: Crocodiles.

The Weakest Link

DJ Mark: For £10, what is the nationality of the Pope?
Ruth from Rowley Regis: I think I know that one. Is it Jewish?

Beacon Radio, Wolverhampton

Presenter: Of which European country is Lisbon the capital?
Contestant: Australia.
Presenter: Sorry, that's the wrong answer; we'll go to the next caller.
Second contestant: I were going to say Australia as well. Is it Gibraltar?

Radio Hallam, Sheffield

Steve Wright: In 1863 which American President gave the Gettysburg Address?
Contestant: I don't know, it was before I was born.

BBC Radio 2

Anne Robinson: In sport, the name of which famous racehorse was the word 'murder' spelt backwards?
Drag queen: Shergar.

The Weakest Link

Sophie Raworth: British politics. Who was the only female member of the Gang of Four?
Contestant: Myra Hindley.

Judgemental, BBC1

William G. Stewart: Which of the Queen's six grandchildren, described as 'a blonde 5'5" knockout', was named this year by the American entertainment magazine People as one of the 50 most beautiful people in the world?
Contestant: Prince Edward.

Fifteen-To-One

Andy Collins: Name something Old Macdonald had on his farm.
Contestant: Giraffe.

Family Fortunes

Les Dennis: Name a type of fork not used for eating.
Contestant: Guy Fawkes.

Family Fortunes

Anne Robinson: According to the common saying, revenge is a dish best served... what? Cold or on toast?
Contestant: On toast.

The Weakest Link

Les Dennis: Name something sold by gypsies.
Contestant: Bananas.

Family Fortunes

Phil Wood: What 'K' could be described as the Islamic Bible?
Contestant: Er...
Wood: It's got two syllables... Kor...
Contestant: Blimey?
Wood: Ha ha ha ha no. The past participle of run...
Contestant: *(Silence)*
Wood: OK, try it another way. Today I run, yesterday I...
Contestant: Walked?

BBC GMR

Anne Robinson: Sancho Panza was the companion of which famous fictional character?
Contestant: Rupert Bear.

The Weakest Link

Daryl Denham: Name Les Dennis's estranged wife.
Contestant: Margaret Thatcher.
Denham: Are you absolutely sure?
Contestant: That's the one.

Virgin Radio

Steve Wright: Which is the largest rodent in North America?
Contestant: The great white whale.

BBC Radio 2

Anne Robinson: According to a poll in Total Guitar magazine, the greatest guitarist of all time was Jimi... who?
Contestant: Savile.

The Weakest Link

Presenter: OK, you say if the following is either alive, dead or Italian food. Giacomo Puccini.
Contestant: Sounds like a type of pasta. Italian food.

Jazz FM Breakfast Show

Anne Robinson: What is the name of the bodily fluid secreted by the lachrymal glands?
Contestant: Semen.

The Weakest Link

Anne Robinson: The equator divides the world into how many hemispheres?
Contestant: Three.

The Weakest Link

Steve Wright: The anchovy belongs to which family of fish?
Contestant: Kipper.

BBC Radio 2

Anne Robinson: The author of *Robinson Crusoe* and *Moll Flanders* was Daniel who?
Contestant: Day-Lewis.

The Weakest Link

Anne Robinson: Which author wrote to a newspaper in 1896 to say that reports of his death had been exaggerated?
Contestant: Jack the Ripper.

The Weakest Link

Anne Robinson: Who was elected leader of the Conservative Party in September 2001?
Contestant: Pass.

The Weakest Link

Steve Wright: Who is the current leader of the Conservative party?
Contestant: Er...

BBC Radio 2

Steve Wright: Who is the leader of the Conservative Party?
Contestant: Er... no... I can't remember.

BBC Radio 2

Anne Robinson: In traffic, what 'J' is where two roads meet?
Contestant: Jool carriageway.

The Weakest Link

Les Dennis: Name something associated with Morris Dancing.
Contestant: Germany.

Family Fortunes

Les Dennis: Name a non-living thing that has feet.
Contestant: A plant.

Family Fortunes

Paul Wappat: How long did the Six Day War between Egypt and Israel last?
Contestant *(after long pause)*: Fourteen days.

BBC Radio Newcastle

Daryl Denham: In which country would you spend shekels?
Contestant: Holland?
Denham: Try the next letter of the alphabet.
Contestant: Iceland? Ireland?
Denham *(helpfully)*: It's a bad line. Did you say Israel?
Contestant: No.

Virgin Radio

Andy Collins: Name a red liquid.
Contestant: Mercury.
Collins: Is mercury red? Let's see if it's there... No, bad luck, I didn't think it was red.
Contestant: I wasn't sure if it was red or green.

Family Fortunes

Anne Robinson: In nature, cumulus and cirrus are types of what?
Contestant: Lion.

The Weakest Link

THE NEOPHILIACS
—— 2002 ——

"Just as grey is this year's black, food is this year's sex."

> Don Grant, *Erotic Review*

"Angling is the new yoga."

> Sam Murphy, *Sunday Times*

"Science... is the new rock 'n' roll."

> David Lister, *The Independent*

"Yes indeed, modern is no longer modern, which means that the past is now the new black."

> Laurence Llewelyn-Bowen, *Daily Express*

"Why cashmere is the new T-shirt."

> Anna Burnside, *Sunday Times*

"History, as they say, is the 'new gardening'."

> Lucy Hodges, *The Independent*

"As one Tory insider puts it, 'Policy is the new black'."

> Ed Vaizey, *Sunday Times*

"Mathilde Seigner shows that fat is the new phwoarr!"

Cosmo Landesman, *Sunday Times*

"Forget comedy, or cooking: nervous breakdowns are the new rock 'n' roll."

Clifford Bishop, *Sunday Times*

"Italian [food] is so last year... Who could have imagined the phrase? Spain is the new Italy. But then who could have guessed that anyone would dare pronounce grey the new black or rocket the new spinach?"

Scotsman

"Kate 'n' Sam have moved there. Liz wants to. The countryside – it's the new black."

Guardian

"Tartan is the new black."

Accountancy Age

"Housework... is the new sex."

Anthea Gerrie, *Sunday Express*

"For Archbishop of Canterbury-elect Rowan Williams, black is the new black. 'Williams wears purple as little as possible,' I'm told."

Charlie Methven, *Daily Telegraph*

Women practise the age old postures of Yoga at a course held at Morecambe Youth and Community Centre, Acre Moss with instruction by Penny Xerri (centre). *–AC20/44V.*

Morecambe Visitor

"When you look at other religions, the practice their way of life and their culture and it doesn't get that much attention but when it comes to Islam everything is blown up.

Evening Advertiser

One promotion for BA's first-class "flying beds" urged "don't stand for sleepless nights". Another said sleep deprivation caused "memory loss, muddled thinking, visual impairment and memory loss".

Grauniad

The scheme will include a Homebase DIY store, Kentucky Fried Children restaurant, car showroom, nine industrial units and 200 parking spaces.

Gloucestershire Echo

MAGGIE: THE FIRST LADY
ITV1, *times vary*
This excellent documentary series reaches its climax tonight as Mrs Thatcher is ruthlessly ousted from power. PAGE 28

The Times

"On a summer evening I stood alone with the Queen Mother on the ramparts of Walmer Castle. Above us flew the standard of the Lord Warden of the Cinque Ports, an office which she wore as gaily as a feather in her hat. Below us, a semicircle of cannon guarded the Kentish coast. She raised her arm and pointed far out across the Channel. 'Look,' she said. 'France.' Within a few days of her 100th birthday, lame and half-blind, she spoke with the voice of King Henry V before Agincourt."

Kenneth Rose, *Sunday Telegraph*

"With the passing of the Queen Mother we have lost our most treasured national person. She was not merely an historical figure. She WAS history... Her friendship was the greatest privilege of my life for which I gave and give thanks every day... May Her Majesty enter into glory in the court of the Lord of Lords and King of Kings."

Lord St John of Fawsley

"What she is interested in at the moment, however, is being the best possible mother to Damian. When I called her up to ask her to dinner last week with a mutual friend, she said she couldn't make it because it was her nanny's night off."

William Cash on Liz Hurley, *Evening Standard*

"Burke's Peerage extends Christmas greetings to all Imperial, Royal and Noble families throughout the world. We wish them a happy, prosperous and secure holiday season, and appreciate the support that they are giving to his Royal Highness al-Sharif Ali bin al-Husain, the future King Ali of the restored Hashemite Kingdom of Iraq."

Harold Brooks-Baker, *Burke's Peerage* Christmas card

"Even before you meet Greg Dyke, you know he's going to be busy. You don't get to be the Director-General of the entire British Broadcasting Corporation by sitting in your office playing Pitch and Putt on your computer all day; you get there by hard work, perseverance and by not being over-enthralled by a good night's sleep."

Paul Walton, *Top Gear* magazine (published by BBC Magazines)

"Rupert Murdoch, the chairman and chief executive of *News Corporation*, the parent company of *The Times*, and his wife Wendi, are expecting their second child. Congratulations."

Andrew Pierce, *The Times*

"Charles Saatchi's ex-wife has warned her successor Nigella Lawson that he's a man who gets crushes and loses interest easily. He's also a collector who has spent his life searching for the perfect piece of art and no doubt the perfect woman. He must be shrewd enough to know that he won't do better than Nigella."

Lynda Lee-Potter, *Daily Mail*

"When he walked out of his bedroom, with his hair pulled back and his skin clear of make-up, my heart lurched. I had been unconsciously prepared for facial scars, even deformity, because of the constant drip-drip of lies and slanders. In fact, his face is strong and serene, and his skin is beautiful – shining, almost translucent. He glows with an aura of energy. His shirt was open, revealing a lithe chest. All the clever words I had rehearsed fell away: I said his name, he said mine and we embraced. I knew at this moment that I had found a lifelong friend."

Uri Geller on Michael Jackson

Pensioner is victim of gang

POLICE believe an organised gang was respon-

Comet, Herts

Sir Nathaniel, a vicar . . . . **PAUL GRUNERT**
Dull, a constable. . . . . **DUNCAN SMITH**

Love's Labour's Lost cast list, National Theatre

TONIGHT

You can make the cremes up to three days ahead: separate the eggs and put the yolks and caster sugar into a large bowl. Cut open the vanilla pods on a white plate and remove the seeds. Scrape the seeds into the egg yolks and sugar and beat to a stiff mixture. Have the spotlessly clean ramekins ready on the roasting pan or tray.

15 • Lancaster 14
14
Blackpool Preston 10 13
Blackburn • Burnley
15 14
Liverpool 10 Bolton Manchester
15
Warrington Altrincham

Lancashire Evening Telegraph

Pseuds
Corner

"[Amanda] Harlech's role at Chanel means she has to spend part of her time living, as Coco Chanel did, in a suite at the Ritz Hotel in Paris. So, when she returns to her family home in Shropshire, it's a chance to completely relax. She gets her hair cut at Nicky Mitchell in Chester, has back manipulation from horse chiropractor Mark Windsor and visits her herbalist Nicky Jevon who concocts creams and essential-oil blends for her and her teenage children, Tallulah and Jassett."

Nova

"Floyer's work in Sunderland is a black bin-liner full of air, slumped on the floor. It reminds us that context and placement is everything, and that the slightest, most abject gesture, can be resonant. Floyer's bag of air makes me think of bodies, futility, emptiness, waste. Its starkness is overwhelming."

Adrian Searle, *Guardian*

"Were it not that I like and respect Andy Marr and believe him to be a force for the good, his march towards interpretative hegemony would terrify me."

Siôn Simon, *Daily Telegraph*

"The expression on [Kevin] Keegan's face is jolting. It is in the eyes, a sadness that no amount of fist-clenching and arm-waving can disguise.

The sadness has been there since Newcastle lost a 12-point lead and a Premiership title. Up till then there had been an aura about Keegan, a sense that come what may, the force of his will would transcend everything. His team lost a championship and he lost more. Art Garfunkel wrote about this in his song 'Bright Eyes':

> Bright eyes,
> Burning like fire,
> Bright eyes,
> How can you close and fail?
> How can the light that burned so brightly
> Suddenly burn so pale?

But football is a street where every second building is a last chance saloon..."

David Walsh, *Sunday Times*

"It's hard to imagine a world without *Marie Claire* these days."

Caroline Roux, *Guardian*

"There are half-formed experiments or slim ideas worked up at soundtracks here [in R.E.M.'s *Reveal*], just 12 highly wrought songs with intriguing lyrics... and tunes whose beauty unfolds slowly over several listens, like flower-heads teased gently open by the sun's rays before bestowing their full glory on the world."

Andy Gill, *The Independent*

"If revisiting all this older male sexual stuff sounds rather laborious, let's just say it is worth reading, if only for those Roth sentences which have the clarity of purpose and elastic muscularity of famished serpents."

Sebastian Smee (reviewing Philip Roth's
new novel), The Spectator

"I'm heading for my summer holiday in Iceland with Emile Durkheim's *Suicide*, E. M. Cioran's *The Temptation To Exist* and Robert Burton's *The Anatomy Of Melancholy*."

Alain de Botton's choice of holiday reading, Observer

"She caused shockwaves as a necrophiliac in 'Kissed'. Now she's back in two new roles – a lap-dancer and a motel clerk who beds all the guests. Molly Parker tells Emma Brockes why these parts will help women gain respect."

Guardian

"Our foremost cartographer of fictional topographies."

Will Self, quoted on the dust-jacket of
Jim Crace's new novel

"Do you know I'm actually quite relaxed about my washing-up liquid? In fact I'm quite attached to its perky, primary gaudiness between the taps. It provides an element of organic uncontrivance in a sea of design control."

Laurence Llewelyn-Bowen, Daily Express

LUVVIES

"Well, I think that Clueless was very deep... I think it was deep in the way that it was very light. I think lightness has to come from a very deep place if it's true lightness."

Alicia Silverstone, *Electronic Telegraph*

"We went somewhere private, and we cried together. It was totally surreal. We sensed a lot of pain in each other. We didn't even really talk. We wrote weird poetry and held each other's hands. It's very weird when your ability to make art from your pain is what brings you fame."

Courtney Love describing a few hours with Russell Crowe, *Bath Chronicle*

"We bought the Buddha recently after spending a couple of weeks with Sting and Trudie in Tuscany."

Anna Friel, *Times Magazine*

"I need to feel people are giving me love. I put out so much love through my work that I feel I have earned the right to expect love or respect in return."

Steven Berkoff, *Teletext*

"My life is the result of a war between destiny and magic."

Iman (Mrs David Bowie), *Mail On Sunday*

His reputation for taking risks precedes him. When he launched his early singing career in New York, he caused a stir by wearing a mask every time he performed. Why? "I wanted to be known for my voice, not some cheap, outward manifestation such as, perhaps, my face."

David Soul, *Mail On Sunday*

"It was incredibly trying on a physical level, but what kept me going was the thought that no matter how difficult it was for me, I knew it had been a lifetime more difficult for Joan."

Milla Jovovich on Joan of Arc, *Evening Standard*

"I'm a great fan of hers, but I haven't read any of her books. I just don't have the time."

Kate Winslet on Iris Murdoch, *Daily Telegraph*

"I think acting is about forgetting yourself in order to give the best of yourself. It's passing through you more than you're creating it. You're not the flower, but the vase which holds the flower."

Juliette Binoche, *Interview* magazine

"We are two people who, despite our celebrity, have remained very simple, very honest and very considerate of others.

We care about the human race. We care about the world."

Catherine Zeta-Jones, *Daily Mail*

You struck gold with Good Will Hunting. *Are you still writing screenplays?*

"I haven't longed to write a screenplay again. I've been writing stuff just personally for me. Just single-word stuff to get me through the day. Sometimes I'll write down just 'root' or 'energy'."

Ben Affleck, *Unreel* magazine

"It's like having a baby, it's like a wedding, it's like suddenly jumping out of a plane."

Tom Hanks, *Guardian Review*

"Actors remind me of soldiers. They're so often sent into battle for hopeless causes, to be stuck on the barbed wire and shot down."

Sir Richard Eyre, *Daily Mail*

"Self-preservation has taught me to moderate what I say. I communicate my passion in a way that takes me on the express train to Pseuds Corner in Private Eye. Acting indulges me. It's my mistress. It's with me in the morning, and puts me to bed at night."

Damian Lewis, *Radio Times*

"It suddenly hit me that even after all these years, I have never really learned how to act. I ran to my trailer and shut the door. I kept saying to myself, 'I want to quit... I want to go home.' And Anthony [Hopkins] knocked at the door and said very calmly, 'It's pretty scary stuff, acting, isn't it?'"

Jennifer Love Hewitt, *Night And Day* magazine

AHOY THERE ... Deputy PM John Prescott takes the helm
AMBITIOUS hairdressers Tracey
Cunningham and Lesley Cooper **Riding wave**

Glasgow Evening Times

The brothers, who work together as widow cleaners, appeared side by side at Furness Magistrates Court.

North Western Evening Mail

INDIA

DELHI without hotels. Try en famille at Tikli Bottom-- airport 45 minutes. Farming, fresh air, walks and hills.

Travel guide

Henman sees balls as key to his success

Driving instructors will no longer ask motorists taking their test to execute three-pint turns

S. Wales Guardian

It's a DUMB DUMB DUMB DUMB world

America

Anne Robinson: Who led the victorious fleet at the Battle of Trafalgar?
Contestant: Horatio Hornblower.

The Weakest Link

Anne Robinson: Aristotle identified four elements. Which of these was denoted by the Greek prefix 'pyro'?
Contestant: Louis Armstrong.

The Weakest Link

Anne Robinson: What 'W' is the capital of Poland?
Contestant: Worcestershire.

The Weakest Link

Host: Name a word that a dog understands.
Contestant: Ruff.

Family Feud (US version of *Family Fortunes*)

Ben Stein: After his abdication, King Edward VIII of England became known as the Duke of where?
Contestant: Duke of Earl.

Win Ben Stein's Money, Comedy Central

Anne Robinson: What was the name of the prison island which closed when the last convicts were transferred in 1963?
Contestant: Australia.

The Weakest Link

Anne Robinson: Which Egyptian actor starred in Lawrence of Arabia and also wrote a newspaper column on the subject of bridge?
Contestant: Naomi Campbell.

The Weakest Link

Jay Leno: Who was the first man on the moon?
College student: Louis Armstrong.

The Tonight Show With Jay Leno

Anne Robinson: Which breakfast pastry is named after the French for 'shape of the waxing moon'?
Contestant: Pop Tart.

The Weakest Link

Anne Robinson: Which former member of the House of Representatives died at the battle of the Alamo?
Contestant: Al Gore.

The Weakest Link

Anne Robinson: What 'H' was the hereditary disease carried by Queen Victoria?
Contestant: Syphilis.

The Weakest Link

Anne Robinson: Which American President wrote more than 30 books, including *Theodore Roosevelt: An Autobiography*?
Contestant: Herbert Hoover.

The Weakest Link

Anne Robinson: Hepatitis is a disease of which organ?
Contestant: The penis.

The Weakest Link

Anne Robinson: In the nursery rhyme, Jack Sprat could eat no what?
Contestant: Grass.

The Weakest Link

Anne Robinson: William Shakespeare wrote seven plays about Kings of England who all shared the same name. What name?
Contestant: Oh... I don't have an answer... *(moment of inspiration)*... Ralph?

The Weakest Link

Australia

Cornelia Francis: The show held annually in London, called Crufts, is for what animal?
Contestant: Sheep.

The Weakest Link

Presenter: For what invention was Sir Frank Whittle best known?
Contestant: Would that be the penknife?

Sydney Radio 2BL 702

Cornelia Francis: When you have completely misunderstood the question, you are said to have got hold of the wrong end of the... what?
Contestant: Dog.

The Weakest Link

Presenter: Which mathematician said, "The most incomprehensible thing about this universe is that it's comprehensible"?
Contestant: Mel Gibson.

Sydney Radio 2BL 702

Presenter: For the prize of this AC/DC album, how do you spell 'AC/DC'?
Martin from Greenwood: Erm... AD/DC. No... yeah! AD/DC.

Local radio, Sydney

Presenter: Who killed Cock Robin?
Contestant: Oh God, I didn't even know he was dead.

The Afternoon Programme, ABC 774

Germany

Sonja Zietlow: What popular chocolate bar was named after the Roman god of war?
Contestant: Snickers.

The Weakest Link

officers noted with alarm that 223 officers and ratings had left the Navy as a result of their homosexuality in the previous three years.

One officer suggested publicising the affairs as a warning to others. "Fleets should be provided with a detailed blow-by-blow account of the Bermuda and Eagle affairs, without mincing the language we use," he said.

Daily Telegraph

The Bush administration plan to immunize 450,000 health care workers against smallpox is getting underway, despite spotty resistance from hospitals and some members of Congress.

USA Today

Janice loves animals and can often be seen walking her west highland terrorist around the ward.

Morecambe Labour Party newsletter

Supermodel harassment charges dropped

Crown Prosecution Service lawyers have dropped charges against a kitchen porter accused of harassing supermodel Claudia Schiffer, it has been announced today.

Daily Telegraph website

● *River rescue partners: Bruce Willis and Sarah Jessica Parker in Columbia's 'Striking Distance'.*

Lichfield Mercury

Warballs

ONE YEAR ON

"[Michael] Schumacher has an extra reason to succeed in Italy – it was at Monza in 2001 that he last failed to finish on the podium. But he admits that the distractions of 11 September meant that winning motor races was not high on his list of priorities. 'It was the reason why I was not on the peak of performance,' added Schumacher, who finished fourth."

BBC News website

"Swindon's traditional diners still have loyal customers. Tina Vogel, 35, manager of Jumbo Snacks in Swindon's market hall, has no plans to close. She said, 'We will always have our regulars. It has been a tough year since 11 September. But the appetite for cooked breakfasts will never die.' Her best seller is the bacon and egg sandwich, at £1.70."

Swindon Evening Advertiser

"After 11 September I'm more passionate than ever to help the American people... When I heard what had happened, I wanted to help at a hospital but realised that as I wasn't a nurse, I'd get in the way."

The Duchess of York in *Good Housekeeping*

"This site is for cat lovers and was started to bring America's cat lovers together after the horrible events on 11 September. If you are a true American cat lover, this is the site for you."

Blurb for *American Cats Co* website

"In the year in which the world was overcome by the tragic events of 11 September and the resulting war in Afghanistan, and George Harrison lost his battle with cancer, a brighter note was struck by Hear'Say, who sold 549,823 copies of 'Pure And Simple' in its first week, a record for a debut act."

Guinness Book Of British Hit Singles

"Al Qaeda Threat Puts Spotlight on Garden Plants"

Headline in *Garden News*

"Alan Hassenfeld, chairman of Hasbro Inc. – a $3 billion international toy company – believes that business is about more than making money. 'For a while after 11 September I questioned whether what we do is meaningful and then I realised that... we're the ones that bring smiles to kids of all ages around the world.'"

Sydney Morning Herald

"Show producer Gil Cates said the Oscars ceremony would go ahead even if the US launches a war against Iraq, but that the tone of the show would 'reflect reality'. Cates warned Oscar winners that the orchestra would strike up to drown out their acceptance speech if they exceeded their 45-second allotment, named more than five people they wanted to thank or produced a prepared script. 'I know they are harsh measures, but they are necessary,' he said."

Guardian

"Hostilities may see demand for luxury stationery increase as people turn to the contemplative act of letter-writing."

Financial Times

"The terrorist seeks to change your way of life. The best way to deal with him is to ignore him and carry on exactly as you would have done in the absence of terrorism. This is a little difficult to do if you have only one Windows system."

Advert for HyperOS Systems in *PC Pro* magazine

"Did you know that the game of rugby will be among those mourning the tragedy of 11 September 2001, a day which saw members of the rugby fraternity among those lost in the plane crashes in New York, Washington DC and Pennsylvania?... As well as the human tragedy of those rugby players lost in the horrific events of that day, the rugby calendar was also shaped by the tragedy, with the Dubai Sevens stripped of its IRB World Sevens Series status, and the Australian Rugby League squad cutting short their tour to the UK."

Planet Rugby website

"Owners of a model village said yesterday they had been forced to delay opening after insurers would not provide cover 'because of a heightened threat from terrorism'. Families will not be able to watch locomotives steam round the 1.5 acres of the miniature landscape at Model Railway Village, Southport, because of the terrorist risk, said owner Ray Jones."

Western Morning News

"Sussex chief constable Ken Jones has made plans on how to police the county if war breaks out in Iraq."

Mid-Sussex Times

"A cat charity [in North London] says fewer people are taking in homeless cats – and they're blaming it on the war in Iraq and congestion charging."

Wood Green Weekly Herald

"The world's most expensive pair of shoes went on sale behind a bulletproof case in Harrods yesterday for anyone with small feet and a spare £1 million. Inspired by the ruby slippers worn by Judy Garland in *The Wizard Of Oz*, and woven with platinum thread and set with 642 rubies, the shoes were designed for an unnamed actress to wear for the Oscars. But Stuart Weitzman, the New York designer, withdrew the size 3½ stilettos as a mark of respect to soldiers fighting in Iraq."

Daily Telegraph

"Thankfully, it now looks as though the war in Iraq is all over bar the shouting. To celebrate this, GYC has decided to make it even easier to book your yacht charter holiday."

Mailing from Global Yacht Charters

THE NEOPHILIACS
—————— 2003 ——————

"WAX TO THE MAX. Is topiaried pubic hair the new pashmina?"

The Times

"Dirty... has become the new clean."
Charlotte O'Sullivan, *The Independent*

"In the vanity stakes, men are the new women."
Channel 4 trail for *Vain Men*

"Is gym the new après-ski?"

Evening Standard

"Is driving the new smoking?"

BBC London News

"Tea-drinking has become the new black."
Catherine Coyle, *The Big Issue in Scotland*

"Boats are the new country cottages."
Evening Standard property supplement

"Is green ink the new red ink?"
Bill Turnbull, *BBC Breakfast*

"Is pink the new blue?"

Evening Standard

"Why 40 is the new 30."

Evening Standard

"60 is the new 40."

Lulu in *Sainsbury's* magazine

"80 is the new 70."

Autocar

"Is poetry the new Prozac?"

Radio Times

"Knitting is the new cocaine."

Esther Addley, *Guardian*

"Sleep is the new sex."

Margaret Carlson, *Time* magazine

"Tattoos are the new sex."

Daily Star

"Underwear... is the new jewellery."

Carole Caplin, *Mail On Sunday*

"Bums have been the new boobs for well over a year now."

Lesley Thomas, *Daily Telegraph*

"Is the North the new South?"

Local Government News

"Bradford... it's the new Leeds!"

Headline in *Bradford Telegraph & Argus*

"Southend, the new Vegas."

The Times property supplement

"Ironing is the new yoga."

Jayne Dawson, *Yorskshire Post*

"Bristol really is the new Hollywood."

Bristol Evening Post

"Dead is the new alive."

Fiona Lawrenson, *BBC Gardeners' World*

"The cafetière is the new teapot."

PG Tips advert

"Tea is the new coffee."

Glamour

"The velour tracksuit is the new pashmina."
Cheryl Knoteh, *Financial Times*

"2005 looks to be the new 2002."
Bill Jamieson, *The Business*

"Sunbeds are the new cigarettes."
Sydney Morning Herald

"Are kids the new adults and adults the new kids?"
Evening Standard

"Celebrity is the new herpes."
Ruby Wax, *Sunday Telegraph*

"Deborah Orr: why vibrators are the new
Tupperware."

Independent front page headline

"Flexibility is the new stability."
Budget analysis by BBC Economics Editor Evan Davies

"Dull is the new interesting."
Jeremy Clarkson, *Sunday Times*

NEW ACCESS FOR STROLLING LOVERS

Mr Martin Deighan & Councillor Fraser Gillies on the new bridge

The Buteman, Rothsay

Pseuds
Corner

"The interchange between these rhythms is complex: the percussion syntax of [John] McGahern's sentences transmits to the most routine actions the beat of an impersonal process and the variations of the human consciousness that modifies it. So we are told: 'Tea was made. Milk and several spoons of sugar were added to the tea and stirred.'"

Seamus Deane, *Guardian*

"Yes... he's almost winsomely naïve in his eclecticism."

Michael Berkeley on Alfred Schnittke,
'Private Passions', Radio 3

"One of the few valid 'lessons of history' is that agglutinative processes always set off fissile reactions."

Felipe Fernandez-Armesto, *The Independent*

"I suppose I have what the French refer to as *les signes exterieures de la richesse*; it's not exactly bling-bling, but I wear an old Rolex, and in winter my overcoat has a mink collar."

Philip Hensher, *The Independent*

"The other week I drank milk for the first time in two years. I hadn't intended to. I thought the glass that one of my daughters had at the table contained horchata, an originally Valencian drink based on chufa, the tuberous roots of a kind of sedge. It is not overdoing it to say that one sip of milk prompted a certain revulsion."

Jonathan Meades, *Independent On Sunday*

"The masterful evocation of an entire social structure through the antics of a few exotic characters imprisoned in a supremely artificial environment reminds me of the way in which Alexander Solzhenitsyn views Soviet Russia through the lens of life in a prison camp for scientists and intellectuals in his 1968 novel *The First Circle*."

Nick Foulkes on 'Are You Being Served?', *Mail On Sunday*

"It actually felt as if something in society shifted."

John Cleese on Halle Berry's Oscar, *Los Angeles Times*

"...isn't this all – I hear you mutter – a little de trop? Well yes, absolutely, and not simply de trop in terms of what we expect from responsible creators, but de trop in terms of Horsley's own highly ductile psychopathology."

Will Self on the artist Sebastian Horsley, *The Independent*

"Cheap Japanese food is a little like masturbation."
Jay Rayner, *Observer Magazine*

"As an historian of sorts, I view clothes and hats as pieces of living history. I live my clothes."
Petronella Wyatt, *Spectator*

"His aunt tells him he spends too much time in his bedroom and fears he might be gay. Stranded in his almost existential isolation, he desires intimacy with the people around him, but spurns contact for fear of imperilling their lives. The trails of sticky webbing that the film shows gushing from his wrists represent the pent-up longing and sorrow of the compulsive masturbator."
Sukhdev Sandhu reviewing 'Spiderman', *Daily Telegraph*

"As anyone who has ever worked as an advisor to a senior politician knows..."

Amanda Platell, *New Statesman*

"I become the sacrifice. I become the building. I become the plane."

Steven Berkoff tells the World Service how he will perform his poem 'Requiem for Ground Zero' at the Edinburgh Festival

"I mention Samuel Beckett's Three Dialogues With Georges Duthuit, which, startlingly, he hasn't read."

Bryan Appleyard interviewing Sir Tom Stoppard, *Literary Review*

"I'm particularly vulnerable to shoes and panties. Lately, I've been obsessed with a rhinestone bikini. I also like different kinds of shoes – I'm really greedy about them. I regard shoes as the cars of women's feet."

Patricia Arquette, *In-Style*

"Last weekend, I did research in my office at home, getting my head around the problems with the NHS – about five years' work in itself."

Nicky Campbell, *Guardian*

"As much as I think I've inspired people in the world and helped people sometimes, and as much as I think I may have done some good in the world, I'd like to be more involved in bringing about world peace."

Madonna, quoted in *Observer*

"This is very highly wrought food. It has the edginess and mild fury of Gordon Ramsay's first two years at Royal Hospital Road..."

Giles Coren, *The Times Magazine*

"I recently did a blind tasting of all the best champagnes of the last century and it was phenomenal the way the Cristal stood out. There is something roguish and mischievous about it that only very stylish people understand."

Serena Sutcliffe, 'Me And My Champagne',
Financial Times Saturday Magazine

"My child was not only carried by me, but by the universe."

Celine Dion, *Radio Times*

Why did we all do so little to prevent human cloning?

The ProLife Alliance's battle against the Human Fertilisation and Embryology Authority has ended in defeat. Josephine Quintavalle asks why Catholics did so little to fight it

The Catholic Herald

I've always been good at juggling a lot of balls in the air, but having fantastic staff helps. And when my balls do drop, my staff are always there to hoover them up.

Cameron Mackintosh, The Independent

IF you enjoy working with people, why not become a mortuary technician?

Dorset Echo

SIMON HEFFER IS AWAY

Great news for people aged 50 and over

Daily Mail

USED CARS – Some points to look for

⚠ **Tyres**
All tyres (including the spare) should have a tread depth of at least 1.6mm and be inflated to the

⚠ **Interior**
Carpets, pedals and the dashboard can be valuable indicators as to the authenticity of the mileage. All show

⚠ **Locks**
Try each lock to make sure that it works. Look out for damaged rubber seals as these can be

⚠ **Engine**
Check the condition and amount of oil as well as the colour of the water in the radiator. Also, listen out for

Yorkshire Evening Press

Warballs

THE FIRST CASUALTIES

"Will Mr Blair be the war's first casualty?"
Mail On Sunday

"Duncan Smith first casualty as skirmishes begin."
The Times

"Cabinet solidarity, war's first casualty."
The Times

"Europe is the first casualty of war."
Financial Times

"The first casualty of war is television ratings."
The Business

"Trees, not truth, are the first casualties of war."
The Times, on the glut of books about Iraq

"My address book is the first casualty of war."
Stephen Pollard, *The Times*

"House prices are the first casualty of war."
The Times

"Comedy series The Sketch Show has become the 'first casualty of war' according to producer Steve Coogan."
The Stage

I'm a celebrity, get me out of DUMB BRITAIN

Chris Tarrant: What is another name for the Pope?
A: Pontiff. B: Pontiac. C: Poncho. D: Pontefract.
Emma Bunton (Baby Spice) and
Will Young (Pop Idol) *(after two minutes)*: We'll
ask the audience, Chris.

Who Wants To Be A Millionaire?, ITV

Contestant (child of ten): Who is the Deputy
Prime Minister?
Brian Dowling (Big Brother winner): William
Hague.
Tess Daly (co-presenter): No it's not, he's the
leader of the opposition.

SMTV Live, ITV

Cosmologist: ...and eventually the star becomes a
red giant, or, if it's a really massive star, a super red
giant.
Melvyn Bragg: Is it called 'red' because of the
colour?
Cosmologist: Erm, yes.

In Our Time, Radio 4

Anne Robinson: Which 'A' is another name for the white of an egg?
Eddie 'the Eagle' Edwards: Yolk.

The Weakest Link

Nicky Campbell: Did Shakespeare ever split an infinitive?
William Shatner: Sure he did.
Campbell: Can you give me an example?
Shatner: To be or not to be.

Radio 5 Live

62 A Life in the Day The man who lives happily with a hippo

Sunday Times

Press Release

"The aggressive 'homosexual lobby' appear to have their fingers into everything" stated a UK LifeLeague spokesman...

UK LifeLeague

7 Reasons Why Teacher's Find Us Top Class.

They hunted in the forests, travelled widely, and had one daughter, Marie-Anna Berta Felicie Johanna Ghislaine Theodora Huberta Georgina Helene Genoveva, known as "Bunny".

The Times

"Officials are pretty terrified around the whole of Europe about how to confront some of these huge vested interests."

Item on obesity, BBC News Website